Where Have All My Metaphors Gone?

~ Memories, Reflections, and Wordplay ~

To Kathy —
Who keeps things
under control —
and gives 'control' a
good name! —
Thanks for everything, Kathy —
Rosemary

Rosemary Sullivan

Where Have All My Metaphors Gone?

Text © Rosemary Sullivan

Design/Art Direction Lisa Breslow Thompson
LisaThompsonGraphicDesign.com

Library of Congress Control Number: 2018943097
ISBN: 9781941573198

Published by Damianos Publishing
1630 Concord Street
Framingham, MA 01701 USA
www.DamianosPublishing.com

Produced through Silver Street Media by Bridgeport National Bindery, Agawam, MA USA

First printed 2018

"Each mortal thing does one thing and the same:

Deals out that being indoors each one dwells;

Selves – goes its self; *myself* it speaks and spells,

Crying *What I do is me: for that I came.*"

Gerard Manley Hopkins

Gerard Manley Hopkins often wrote that poetry, to be fully appreciated, should be read aloud. Maybe he reasoned that only then can the resonant sounds, the alliterations, the meter, and inflections be heard. Yes, when you read it, the mind's ear can help, but it is not the same. Imagine taking a piece of music and carefully noting the words, the notes, and the rhythm signs. Without the melody, the sung words, and the actual rhythm, it would be difficult to enjoy it to the fullest. The same logic could apply to poetry.

~ *Dedication* ~

For my daughters,
Kathy, Michaela, and Mary Ellen

and

in memory of my parents,
Kate and Harold Grunert

.

~ *Gratitude* ~

In 2004 the Winchester Public Library sponsored a Year of the Poet. Various activities included a town-wide reading of favorite poems, readings by known and unknown poets, lectures, and workshops. I attended the four-week poetry writing workshop led by Moira Linehan Ounjian. After four weeks, several of us wanted to continue, and continue we did – some of us for twelve years. We called ourselves the Waterfield Poets.

Most of these poems were written during the workshop. My thanks go to my fellow poets: Rino diBartolo, Sara Epstein, Pamela Fishman, Bill Mallio, Scott Meeks, Anne Murray, and Dave Powell, for their companionship, advice, and encouragement, and, of course, Moira Linehan Ounjian, (don't tell me, show me!) for her caring leadership.

Many thanks go to Martha O'Neil for her cover design and technical assistance. I am grateful to my readers, Pam McAneny and Bill Mallio, for their kind and valuable suggestions. Special thanks also go to my brother, Bill Grunert, who has been an unacclaimed "reader" over the years, as well as an able advisor and a caring confidante.

~ Contents ~

Memories

Reflections

Persona

Wordplay

~ *Memories* ~

Heading Home

July arrives, and I must head for home.
Home? Fifty summers since, a state away,
by car, six pleasant picture-postcard hours.

Haphazard, helter-skelter hills become
stoic, Stone-age mountains which descend into dallying valleys.
Valleys then claim their unrivaled rights to the river.

Sporadic scene-spoiling, sprawling factories
may flaw the river's noble flow,
until finally farm country commands the lush and lavish land.

Pristine pastures, wooden fences corralling casual cows,
checkerboard fields boasting an occasional barn and silo,
and the ever-remembered "essence of agriculture" –
all tell me that I'm home!

My Town

My town was small ... important, but not renown –
Small – unless you think 4,000 people make a multitude.

State Street started at the 'Town Limits' sign
and descended into the valley that was our downtown,
then climbed the hill to the General Hospital –
where you saw the other 'Town Limits' sign.

Between the signs were important buildings,
My town was the County Seat – meriting a Court House.
The new Court House was built when I was seven –
boasted Greek architecture – four large three-story pillars,
and then, the only elevator in the county.

Across the street, the new Post Office was constructed
when I was ten.
It had granite blocks in the front sidewalk.
It was like roller skating on velvet
and gave my skates a wonderful, whirring sound.

The school had always been there, looking like a giant gray brick.
The lavish lawn hosted high school band concerts.
The 'brick' had five doors, each for a certain grade section.
Seniors swaggered in the front door, with the teachers.
Over the door was engraved, 'Enter to learn, go forth to serve.'

Our traffic light was downtown – at the four corners.
It directed the shoppers as they moved from store to store,
buying meat for stews, looking for shoes, catching up on the news ...
unless something special was needed.

A party dress might require a family trip to the city.
I loved the city, but on the way home my father said,
"It's a nice place to visit, but I wouldn't want to live there."
We all agreed with him.

The Crosswalk

The first day I walked alone to school,
I had to cross a very busy street.
Officer Gerry stretched out his arms
and cheerfully nodded for me to cross.

Later that day he left his post
to visit our classroom.
He explained that we could safely cross,
if only we stayed within the crosswalk lines.

I remember feeling so elated in my classroom,
assured that I would be safe from harm,
and could walk happily and safely within the lines,
shielded by my six-year-old sense of security.

Seven decades later and better acquainted with harm,
I return to the same street and the school,
trying not to yearn for that feeling of security
I felt at the crosswalk, when Gerry stretched out his arms.

Walking with a Nun

In memory of Sister Mary Hortense Cavanaugh, S.S.J.

It was fun to be walking with a nun
My mother's sister, "sister" by name, aunt to me
Austere black habit, starched white wimple, daunting to some,
   special to me
– 'Does she really stay at your house?'

It was fun to be visiting a nun
Everything convent-clean, stained-glass beautiful, familiar to me
Bustling black habits, well-worn prayer books, reassuring to me
– 'What can go wrong while they're praying?'

It was fun to be walking with a nun
Burly men with soft smiles, remembering someone who taught them
   a prayer...
Business men, carrying files, reminded of one who insisted they care.
– 'Sister, is that really you after all these years?'

It was fun to be walking with a nun –
Walking and talking and listening and laughing,
Knowing that she was special ... making me feel special.
– 'So, what do you want to be when you grow up?'

County Fair
A Northern New York Summer Event

All year long we waited for the first week in August,
Saved our coins, and made our plans.
Farm folks prepared their vegetables and groomed their livestock.
Women baked apple pies and bottled sweet pickles.

Then came the trucks ... out of the night, into our town.
Almost a block long, noisily shifting their gears.
I could only imagine what magic was inside.
Was it the carousel, or maybe an untamed tiger?

We walked furtively past the fairgrounds the next day.
Peered through peepholes in the fence for a glimpse of glitter –
Baseball throws, bingo, ring toss, glitzy games ...
And the kewpie doll prizes – which would we choose?

Sometimes we would watch the workers leaving the grounds –
So mysterious! Would he be running the ferris wheel?
The next person might be a clown or an acrobat!
That woman had to be a trapeze artist!

Finally – Opening Day!
Which ride? What game? Where to go first?
The music of the carousel seemed to spread over us like a tent.
The hot dogs, pop corn, cotton candy, sausages were everywhere –
smells only smelled the first week of August.

Sugar on Snow

There was a language: the maple forest was the "sugar bush."
In early spring the trees were "tapped" for the sap;
the sap was boiled in the "sugar shanty."
The whole process was called "sugaring off."

But what we waited for was "sugar on snow."
The conditions had to be just right:
warmer days, colder nights, and fresh snow,
fresh snow that was tamped down in dishpans.

My grandfather always presided. We watched
as the kettle of brown syrup went from frothy bubbles
to a thick satiny simmer, filling the air with maple.
Then, armed with our forks, we waited.

We watched as the large spoon of drizzled syrup
became ribbons of maple caramel on the packed snow.
Then we wound the ribbons around our forks
and let the pure, exquisite maple nuggets melt in our mouths.

Adults and children savored this family ritual,
which took place once every spring. I tried to repeat it
for my children, but sadly, conditions weren't right.
Boiled maple syrup poured on ice cubes just doesn't make it.

Leaf Celebration

Walking home from school,
wading through a sea of ankle-high leaves,
swish, swishing through dots of rust, yellow, and brown.
Clearly, the time was here to get out the rakes
and get ready for our annual Leaf Celebration.

Heaps of leaves soon became leaf hills, which
then became leaf mountains, leaves
which swirled themselves into
mammoth leaf monsters, begging to be attacked.

One by one,
we got a running jump
and dove into the mountain
of leaves, immersing ourselves
in a crispy, crackly, crunchy cloud, carefully
closing our eyes, also our mouths to avoid a leaf lunch.

Such a feeling of freedom and movement, without
fear of falling, – of being off the ground, but yet grounded!
Such a feeling of power, importance!
Knowing that when our mountain grew smaller, in seconds
we could restore and rebuild an even bigger mountain!

Eventually the jumpers were tired and the leaves were tattered.
It was time to rake the leaves over to the end of the driveway
And watch as our mountain of leaves became a giant bonfire.
Flames flared, emitting little fireworks against the darkening sky.
The special smell of burning leaves meant that the season was over;
Leaf Celebration would come again next year.

Adirondack Acrophobia

My hometown was small, but I loved to "take to the woods" –
woods that were deep and dense, and smelled like balsam pillows.
In my teen years, I loved camping with my friends –
with time to explore, look for an occasional deer, or
jump in the lake, where we had once seen a swimming moose.

One damp day – a day more for hiking than swimming,
someone remembered the Forest Ranger tower nearby.
And there it was – a small glass room standing on stilts,
reaching to the sky. And there was the Ranger, smiling down,
granting us permission to climb up the diagonal ladder-stairs.

Four scrambled up the ladder, soon viewing mountains of trees;
I was middle-mired, unable to move up or look down.
Panic may have mangled the memory of those moments, but
the horror I felt, creeping down, has kept me grounded for life.

Pastel Icicles

Anyone who says movies have never been better
has not had the "movie plus live show" experience,
when the movie was the prelude –
when Joan Crawford or Bette Davis were tolerated
until the stage came alive!

My first live show was preceded by Doris Day –
Doris Day in a pillbox hat, a sailor suit, in rapture, in tears,
Doris doing mistaken identity, Doris doing time,
and, finally, Doris beaming through her tears – and freckles.

The unending credits, then the theater went black.
Suddenly a wall of bright, shimmering pastel icicles appeared on stage.
A hush went through the theater as people waited ...
then the lush sounds of saxophones brought in
the strains of *Getting Sentimental Over You,*
as Tommy Dorsey's trombone softly sealed his signature.

The wall of icicles lifted, replaced by shining brass.
A sea of horns, filled the stage – swaying slightly.
Muted tones brought forth *Stardust, Opus One, Tangerine, and Marie.*
Reeds flirted with brass, brass went staccato, the game reversed.
Bass and snares played backup, opting for a solo here and there.
Pulses quickened as the piano belted out Boogie Woogie.

Audience and band became one – bound together by the beat
and the love of the wonderful mellow sound
emanating from the large ensemble on stage.
Nobody knew it was what history would call the Big Band Era.
We just knew we hated to see those pastel icicles descend.

Seven Years

It was a lovely summer scene –
packing up the car for a Cape vacation –
Two chattering little girls and a baby girl, three months old.
Her entourage: portacrib, nip and nap, blankets, and bottles,
all carrying that sweet baby smell.

And, best of all, an adoring grandmother
to happily lavish love on baby while
others scrambled off to the beach –
the beach – home to crabs, shells, and sand dollars,
provider of building material for numerous castles and moats.

Then back to the cottage for showers and hamburgers,
planning the trip to my brother's September wedding,
enjoying our rather passive role of groom's family,
mostly concerned with coordinating colors, and such fluff.

The evening knock at the door prompted puzzled, uneasy looks.
More uneasy when we saw two policemen –
still more uneasy when they asked for my mother.
Her suddenly thin voice inquiring, "Is it Harold?"
My father had chosen to remain at his retirement job,
rather than join the family fun this time.

Telephone calls, arrangements, bits of information,
arrangements, more calls, and questions – most unanswered.
Images of my father, fallen with a stroke,
inching his way to the telephone,
now at least safe at the hospital.

Safe? The once-tan face blends into the white sheets now.
The hearty laugh has become a forced, uncertain smile.
Speaking in a small voice, he says he is fine
and tries to tease me, but we are relieved when he just rests.

Continued on next page

Watching him, the picture blurs.
I see a man getting out of his car, fishing pole in hand,
proudly displaying speckled trout, then proceeding to fry them.
Or I am waiting for the car to pull into the driveway.
Finally it does – with a deer languidly lounging on the front fender.

Equilibrium – it doesn't mean much, unless you don't have it.
After the stroke, my father didn't have it –
something about his Circle of Willis,
and the flow of blood to his brain.
What it really meant was seven years in a nursing home.

Seven years of visits in April and July –
April, when he blew out his birthday candles
with our youngest daughter – who shared his birthday.
Seven years of lessening eye contact, brought on by lessening recognition.
Did my daughters not realize the truth, or were we pretending for each other?

Sometimes we opted for an October visit –
And one October ... all recognition had gone,
then my father left –
Once again the telephone calls, arrangements, questions, more arrangements –
and then it was over.

Driving the 310 miles home, I allowed myself to confront the seven years.
For the first time, I viewed them as I would a documentary.
It was about a life that had drastically changed,
and how everybody, including that life, learned to cope.
It was like living on a continuum: sometimes less sad, sometimes more sad.

Then I slowly slid off the continuum.
No purpose would be served by staying.
My father, with his sad eyes and freeze-frame body, was gone.
The picture blurs and he emerges from his Bel Air Chevy, Met Life
    book under his arm,
winking, and asking if Mom has made a blackberry pie for dinner.

My Mother's Visit

My mother came to visit me last night.
Now as I ease away from hazy sleep,
I linger on a peaceable plateau
and let my random thoughts fall into play.

My mother came to visit me last night.
I always plan her sojourns weeks ahead.
My guest room houses my computer now –
'What will they think of next?' my mom will say.

My mother came to visit me last night.
That means our morning coffee once again
and stories from the town where I grew up,
told in my mother's impish, witty way.

My mother came to visit me last night.
I listen for some sound that she's awake.
Impatient, I go back to planning mode –
just how to use this long-awaited day.

My mother came to visit me last night.
She has, no doubt, a project for this trip –
cleaning cupboards, maybe sorting herbs,
her way of helping out during her stay.

My mother came to visit me last night.
She'll want a day to browse the city shops.
She'll say her wardrobe needs a little lift,
somehow my closet always carries sway.

Last night my mother came to visit me.
Her smile, her laugh, her fragrance – here again.
She'll bask in every word of family news –
I have so much to tell her, much to say.

Farming the Winds

Remote reaches of land on Tug Hill,
tucked away in northern New York State.
Once known but to a native few,
suddenly now a world-famous wind farm.

Once only known for blustery winter chill,
for howling winds, refusing to abate,
for summer breezes, drinking morning dew,
ever blowing wayward, wanton, and warm .

Now slender giants rise up from the hill.
Majestic arms reaching over the state,
noble towers once witnessed by a few,
until the world found out about this farm.

Through winds of summer's heat and winter's chill,
The gracious circling arms do not abate,
Producing power as they were built to do,
Brought on by icy gales and breezes warm.

Moving Day

I stand at center stage, otherwise known as the doorway,
of my large, comfortable, Dutch colonial home,
my faithful partner in providing refuge for 29 years,
now falling prey to the demon, downsizing.

The cavernous van with its gaping mouth
has already swallowed much of my furniture.
My mother's Hoosier cabinet will surely feel like a country bumpkin
in sophisticated Brooklyn Heights.

The quarter-sawn oak hutch my grandfather made will cringe
to be housing a Barbie boutique, instead of linens and crystal.
And the staid New England marbletop table
will never feel quite at home in trendy San Francisco.

Boxes leave my house on a conveyor belt made of four strong backs,
backs housed in muscle-bulging tee shirts, stating 'Carefree Carriers."
Soon all my books, china, my homemaking tools will be unwilling refugees,
getting established with me in a new land.

I glance back at the carefully chosen wallpaper, the now-naked windows,
the fruitwood beams I will never dust and de-web again.
And, like an actor on the last night of the best play,
I say to myself, "It was a very good run."

Moving the Miracle Machine

Behold the Jenks miracle machine!
Large, complex, unique, beautiful to see,
amazing when operating on track at full speed,
which is most of the time.

This complicated creation is made up of 150 moving parts,
bound together by a sense of purpose and commitment glue.
Most of the parts are mature, but in good condition.
Occasionally a weak cog has to be replaced,
or a broken axle must have time to mend,
but the remaining parts cover the situation
and the operation proceeds as usual.

My job: to watch this wondrous machine
as it moves from Point A to Point B.
Fend off floods, fools, foes, and frauds,
and field a fine fiscal formula.
Time allowed for the move: two years.

Perks of my job: Being one of the 150 movable parts,
being able to monitor the machine in motion,
observing the machine serve its movable parts,
working with the other local machines,
– and beholding the miracle.

Reluctant Truckers

Rolling along on Interstate 80,
daughter at wheel, mom riding shotgun,
hauling a car perched on an auto-transport,
trucking from California to New England.

An unlikely duo on this busy highway,
housed in the cab of a fourteen-foot van,
wedged in between them sat Apprehension,
watching and waiting to take command.

While ascending the Mountains Sierra,
Apprehension seemed to be gaining ground.
What could be causing those strange engine sounds?
What could be making the floorboards so hot?

Rain pelted down without any warning.
Was the auto-transport flashing red lights?
Was the transport beginning to pull to one side?
Then Apprehension took over the wheel.

Suddenly we were approaching an exit,
leaving the highway to wind and to rain,
knowing we were on uncharted routes now,
hoping that we hadn't gone the wrong way.

Never a lodge so gratefully welcomed.
Campers and truckers lined up for rooms.
Too wet and too washed out to take notice
Of the huge double rainbow that covered the sky –

Or the name of the heaven-sent haven.
But on the next morning – so clear and pristine,
we glanced back at our rescuing refuge,
and there was the name – Donner Pass Lodge.

The River

The river was definitely a plus
when I was weighing the reasons to buy my condo ...
thirty feet from my door,
flowing slowly, steadily, toward the center of town,
so serene, so scenic, so rustic!

Getting settled, I sometimes stole time for a short walk
along the path beside the water.
Short bushes and thin trees on the riverside,
huge pine trees on the side toward my place,
spaced to allow a good riverview.

Gradually the river became a part of my setting –
my backdrop, background, my animated art.
Always there, meandering along, rising with the rainfall,
receding with the dry spells –
oblivious, adrift, and independent.

One day, needing a subject for a poem,
I wandered down to the pine needle path.
Walking along the river again was pleasant,
revisiting something that had always been there ...
So perfectly natural.

Bushes arching gracefully over the water,
shrubs gone wild, wedging between thin trees –
all vying for reflection
in the mirror surface of the now tranquil river,
until a soft wind changed the mirror to crinkled cellophane.

I gathered in these familiar views,
feeling both the contentment of the known,
and the excitement of rediscovery – or was it discovery?
Had I ever looked at the river in just this way?

The river became a viable part of my landscape.
Opened blinds now made it a part of my room,
reflecting the morning sun in shades of pink and yellow,
or silver ripples at night, enhanced by a streetlight-moon.
With all this awareness, it had become a part of my life.

And so with you, my friend,
so many years, dwelling in my background,
and now a part of my life.
Still independent, but not oblivious, not adrift,
just perfectly natural.

Fire!

I imagine the sound of the fire siren rounding the corner near my house,
  And I didn't even hear it.

I imagine the firemen leaping off the truck and opening the gushing
  fire hydrant,
  And I didn't even feel the mist.

I imagine the folded hoses spilling from the fire truck,
  And I didn't even see them.

I imagine being at my daughter's house and the 12:30 AM phone call –
  But I did hear that – and the message from my son-in-law to my daughter,
  "They said to prepare her." I'll always hear that.

One-half hour of imagining what I would see, until we finally drove up
  to my smoldering house.

The horizontal ladder (ladders should be vertical)
  Going from the fire truck to my bedroom window
  (Are the firemen walking across my bed?)

The crowd of people gaping at the flames coming from the roof, my roof –

Voices in the crowd: "Here's the owner – let her through."

My neighbors – some rushing over, some crying, some wearing brave smiles.

Voice of the captain, "It's really not as bad as it looks."
  (It looks terrible!)

Voice of another fireman, "We were able to save most of the family pictures that were hanging on the walls. They're in your sunroom." (How were they able to find them?)

At 3:30 AM I walk through my house on water-soaked rugs, heavy smoke still lingering.
  The rooms look like smudged charcoal drawings of my home.

I find that the damage is confined to the back wall of the house, as I look through the burned-out hole in my daughter's closet to my back yard.

I find that the fire was set by an arsonist at my back door with an undetermined accelerant.

Six months later I find that a house, like the phoenix, can rise from the ashes.

October Afternoon

... an acrostic poem from "worlds of wanwood leafmeal lie"
"Spring and Fall to a Young Child"
Gerard Manley Hopkins

Walk with me in Sudbury fields
On this opalescent October day.
Rays from the sun seem to sear,
Lessened by the gentle rush of wind,
Dancing around us as we dawdle –
Shameless in our purposeless meandering.
Only the perfection of this amazing day
Frees us to yield to the moment.

Wandering into a woods-room, our ceiling is
Awash with Seurat-like dots –
Nubs of orange, magenta, and gold.
Wiping out the brilliant blue sky,
Ousting any seeping sunlight,
Opaque and enveloping,
Decorating our world with an ochre glow.

Leaves drop like diffident details,
Earthbound, freefalling, adrift,
Afloat, then becoming petals strewn across our path,
Fashioning a carpet as we amble along the lane,
Mish-mashing through the crumbling leaves.
Eager now for open fields, warm sun, and wide sky,
At last we emerge from our leafy lair,
Languishing in the pure radiance of the cloudless sky.

Lying on the still-soft grass, gazing up
In order to embrace the panorama above us, we are
Ever in denial that this dazzling day will end.

Watch the Rain

Watch the rain fall as the river rises.
Watch each drop shoot down from the gray, murky sky,
piercing a hole in the waiting water,
sending out hundreds of overlapping circles.

See how the river eagerly gathers the drops,
gulping greedily, growing, widening,
no longer wandering, but whirling,
surging, savoring its power.

Watch my watery window
as thousands of tiny streams race down the pane
making the tall evergreens and the gray sky outside
a ghostly, forbidding watercolor.

Listen to the constant cadence of the marching rain
on the roof, on the patio, on the garden.
Watch, as the river overtakes its bank.
Watch the tall evergreens rising from the water.
Watch the river, pushing toward my patio.

~ *Reflections* ~

The Lost
A Pantoum

One time-study says
we spend one-fifth of our lives
looking for lost articles.
Important items just disappear.

We spend one-fifth of our lives
searching for the misplaced.
Important items just disappear.
Our birth certificates, passports – our identities!

Searching always for the misplaced,
that Christmas card with the check,
our birth certificates, passports, free passes,
the receipt for the defective toaster,

The Christmas card with the check–
did we check the trash barrel?
Where's the receipt for the defective toaster?
Did we already trash the waste baskets?

Should we check the trash barrel –
or get on with the other four-fifths of our lives?
Just trash all the waste baskets,
spurn the study, and pray to St. Anthony.

Timing is Everything

Split-second timing often seals your fate.
A moment lost or gained can change a plan.
It's more than being early or too late.

Split-second timing often holds your fate.
The subway door shuts even though you ran.
So went the interview that wouldn't wait.

Timing can really get you in a state.
The parking spot you missed would have been grand,
and, yes, it was a long-awaited date.

Timing can intimately bend your fate.
That backward glance after the room you scanned;
the eye contact that led you to your mate.

Who doesn't question timing with some hate?
The intersection with the speeding van –
survive by being early – or too late.

So learn to conquer time, no time to wait!
Maneuver minutes – make a foolproof plan.
Split-second timing will *not* seal your fate –
When you learn how, will it be too late?

A Leap of Faith

Butch Cassidy diving into the gorge,
Evel Knievel flying over countless cars,
George H. W. Bush jumping out of a plane –
one thing in common – great leaps of faith

Knowing the river might hide a boulder,
the motorcycle could fail in flight,
the parachute might opt not to open –
How to deal with these grim contingencies?

And what about the less dramatic?
Inching a car between six-foot snowbanks at a 4-way?
Braving the NYC traffic during rush hour?
Two women driving a 14-foot van across the country?
Less dramatic – no less real.

Bringing my grandson to his driving test,
seeing his excitement, his eagerness to get behind the wheel,
trying to tune out potential crazies, hazardous roads, unbridled zeal,
seeking assurance that he would elude possible peril –
What to do? Where to go? Nowhere! No assurance!
To live is to take that leap.

Reunion

The journey had been planned for years.
Friends assembled at a mid-state junction
to sojourn north to attend a function
a weekend of happy tears and cheers.

Shared hysteria followed declared history.
Crises, crusades, and accomplishments
evoked dismay, delight and astonishment.
The magic of this mesh remains a mystery.

To: Jane Hirshfield

About her poem: *It was Like This: You Were Happy*

Your poem made me say yes ...
Made me wonder if it were a revelation,
Or something I had always known – a little,
Or had not acknowledged – completely.
It was like that – an epiphany.

It was about this – coming to terms with your life,
the good, the bad – the happy, the sad.
But accepting all of it as your life
and loving it because it is yours.
Your poem made me say yes!

Others cannot explain you, or even understand you.
They offer their version of you – as they see you ...
Someone twice removed from who you truly are.

It was about this – cherish your life each day.
Wear it proudly, wrap it around you.
Let it keep you warm.
Know that each thread was woven in for a reason,
and the loom belongs to you.

Thinking about Billy Collins

I linger over the memories,
the excitement of his town visit,
the cocktail party, the reading,
the book signing, my groupie exhilaration,
his secrets of creativity,
his need to be gazing out a window,
the shocking revelation that he spends just one day on a poem.

Remembering how I discovered him –
requesting a 'man's poet' – and then
immediately connecting to his work –
to his self-indulgent whimsy,
his often humorous musings,
sometimes bordering on the pretentious –
but consistently, in his style, honest.

Perhaps some of his charm has diminished, but ...
I still chuckle as I read *Nightclub*
get a catch in my throat when I walk *The Iron Bridge*
and wish I had known *The History Teacher.*
I still read *The Lanyard* to my daughters on Mother's Day,
and totally relate to the message in *Forgetfulness.*
I guess the connection is still there.

The Journey

Tell me about your journey, John.
Did the path have twists and turns?
Or was it short and clearly marked?

Skywriting over the sea?
Stark words carved on a mountain?
Messages you could not miss?

Maybe it was like a puzzle ...
a careless clue here or there –
begging investigation?

Were you detained by detours –
distracted by detractors –
demoralized by doubters?

When you knew the truth at last,
was it a sudden certainty –
Or a soft, slow permeation,
like a warm, wet summer rain?

But did any of that really matter,
when you walked from Eastern Bank
into your Jesuit life?

Two-Family Dance at Long Nook

Massive dunes diminished only by the daunting sea,
sentinels watching the ever-approaching waves,
standing guard over sun lovers, sand lovers, sand castles –
meeting the sun each morning, greeting the horizon.
Long Nook, the most beautiful of beaches.

For us it was a symbol – our vacations at the Cape!
We knew the routine: our two-family dance.
Pick a time, pack the car, over the bridge,
meet for burgers at PJ's – we were a team!
The routine continued – unpack the car, get a sticker,
load the gear, then off to the shore!
The diagonal path descending to the beach,
chairs and umbrella in tow – and there we were,
seeking the sandbars and searching for sand dollars.

It seemed that it would go on forever,
My brother and I bringing our families to the Cape, but –
years of nor'easters challenged the stalwart dunes.
Years of performance had altered our two-family dance.
New members and a new generation of beach lovers,
all brought new steps, new rhythms, new routines.
Exciting, but sometimes challenging to adapt.
But we must keep revising the choreography.
We have the stage – Continue the dance!

Thanksgiving 2014 – Marshfield

Cursing the Campaigns

Slams and slurs from mouths of fools,
Character assassins' tools.
Barbs and blows designed to bruise,
Bludgeoning the evening news.
Acid rots a reputation,
Feed it to a wary nation.
Polls may change with every ration,
Rancor rolls from every station.
Spewing venom, sowing doubt,
Trashing names, abusing clout.

Slams and slurs from mouths of fools,
Character assassins' tools.
Pushing poison, unveiling vice,
Supreme ruling bars no price.
Rotting lies begetting smears,
Feeding into fractious fears.
Malice, hatred, fear, and spite –
Cram the airways every night!
Defile, degrade, detract, deride
Dehumanize the other side.
Sully, stain, and tarnish names.
Debase them with some baseless claims.

This country fought for these elections
And now must suffer vile defections.
Slams and slurs from mouths of fools –
Character assassins' tools.

The Origin of My Name

In faraway northern New York
in a one-room country school,
my mother taught eight or ten students –
whatever grades were needed in a given year.

During the week she lived in
a country hotel, located squarely
in the middle of nowhere – accommodating
lumbermen, farm equipment salesmen,
deer hunters from the "city," (Natives beware!)
and sometimes the local school teacher.

The proprietors, Rose and Orey Monnat,
provided homey rooms, delicious meals,
and a convivial "taproom," echoing the Wayside Inn.
Rose became my mother's dear friend, sister, and mother.
Eventually she became my godmother.

As a child I loved those trips to the country,
Rose's big bear hug greetings,
the fascination of her older children,
the simple joy of two families getting together.
In a small way, it made up for my grandmother, Mary –
a person I loved just from hearing about her,
who had left this world before I entered.

Reflecting on Fear

Once in the time of war,
a president told his people
they had only to fear fear itself.

Only in the time of war?
Only what kind of war?
Only what kind of fear?

Fear can generate a war within,
But that can also be a good thing.

Fear can be a guide or a protector.
It can save you from stepping out into busy traffic,
or stepping into a doomed relationship,
or not.

Been through a personal crisis lately?
Fear was probably the precursor,
or prompted the leftover bruises.
or both.

I sometimes reflect on the past fears in my life –
the times I was truly afraid of something: the dark,
of failing an exam, of having cancer, of nuclear war,
afraid for my unborn baby,
afraid the bad guys would win …
– But that is only when I want to punish myself.
Not often.

My father feared and despised spiders.
He said when he was at hunting camp one morning,
he put on his boot and a surprised spider bit him.
It was so painful he couldn't hunt until the afternoon.
That afternoon he was surprised by a bear,
and had to shoot it, although his quest was deer.

I brought all my friends to view the beast in our garage,
until a fellow hunter hauled it away to make a rug.
But my father feared spiders.

The Accident

You're driving down the road – and then you're not.
Like a baby, your eyes droop, quiver, and close,
and suddenly you hit a brick wall –
Only it's a tree – and there goes baby, passenger, and all.

Wake up! Look around! Your passenger is napping!
The cradle is rocking – the bough is breaking – Get out!
The will to live, the struggle to save – Are babies born with it?
Or do rocking cradles and breaking boughs bring it?

Sudden energy, superhuman strength, dragging, pulling –
just dire determination to escape the tinderbox ...
Keep inching away, keep going! At last, both safely away –
and then – the cradle explodes!

Labels

"Depression baby," my daughters call me when I stock up
before a storm, or save leftovers from dinner.
"You never know," I say – not really remembering
the depression years or any horrible hardships endured.
Nor did I cheer for Charlie Chaplin, applaud Alka Seltzer,
or wait by the wireless while Kate Smith sang 'God Bless America.'

My mother was a "turn of the century" baby,
always feigning horror when "1899" appeared on her birthday cake.
The Great Blizzard blew in five months
before my mother arrived, with Montana at minus 60.
Boston was proud to produce the first auto repair shop.
The New York newsboys went on strike from mid-July
to late August, never guessing that they would be glorified
in a Broadway musical called "Newsies," in 2012.

So Completely Human

Start the car, start the radio,
eavesdrop on a commentary already started
about a novelist whose life has ended.

Tributes tumble over the airways,
all the attributes an author could hope for,
but the final words – "he was so completely human."

"So completely human" – meaning what –
better than incompletely human?
much better than completely inhuman.

How did his characters reflect his humanity?
Were they vulnerable, pitiable? Certainly likable …
Certainly people you would want to take a walk with,
have a cup of coffee with, have a talk with?

Or were they admirable, but challenged …
challenged beyond human limitations …
limited, but still unbelievably human?

What made the author so completely human?
Overdoing, overdosing, overcoming?
What made *him* admirable? Or likable?

Just what qualities make a person human?
How do you measure the depth or determine the degree?
Is being so completely human always a good thing?

On the Raft with Huck and Jim

One year my book club decided to
revisit the classics, rereading favorites.
Each month we read a different book.
Each month we had a different discussion leader.
I volunteered to lead *The Adventures of Huckleberry Finn,*
though thinking myself a slacker for having chosen
a book I understood perfectly in the eighth grade.

My eighth grade was in a very small, very neat town:
Four thousand people, five Protestant churches, and one Catholic.
I never wondered where our seven Jewish citizens worshipped.
Segregation was a word seldom used – no need to.
Sometimes I saw "colored people" in a nearby city.
So – literature was an open door, offering new experiences –
The excitement of *Treasure Island,* the majesty of *Ivanhoe,*
The pranks of *Tom Sawyer* and the humorous escapes of Huck Finn –
Fun, romantic, entertaining – completely removed from reality.

Flash forward! I'm reading Huckleberry Finn in my golden years...
I don't remember Huck's neglect and abuse from his father.
Had I actually read about his hunger and his beatings?
The trip down the river on the raft with Jim –
The moment Huck had to decide if he would follow the law
and report kindly Miss Watson's runaway slave,
or risk going to jail for helping Jim escape to his freedom.
Then it was clear –Jim was more moral
than any of his captors – and his freedom was worth the risk!

Continued on next page

What lack of understanding had clouded my eighth grade mind?
How could I have missed the stark reality of the message?
Was the cruelty and racism too harsh for my small-town psyche?
Years later I would see two college friends tearfully part at graduation,
because their own small towns would not abide a mixed-race couple.
I would see an excellent black woman leave her job,
because she felt stereotyped and minimized by her color.
The Good Life for a person of color has improved over the years –
but like Jim's freedom, it remains elusive.

*   *   *   *   *   *   *

Years later when I was teaching literature in middle school,
I argued with my fellow teachers who wanted to impress parents
with a curriculum rich in classics, but too rich for immature minds.
Don't meet Holden Caulfield until you can know him
as more than a precocious preppie, I begged.
Don't try to understand Ethan Frome until you can fathom
desperation and love greater than life itself.
Don't let Huck Finn be just another version of Tom Sawyer.

Because that first meeting may be the only meeting –
unless your book club revisits the classics.

Refracted River

A wide satin ribbon of sunlight flows across my ceiling.
Mesmerized by its constancy, I watch the watery path
as it glides from east to west, across the room.
Although the movement is steady, the patterns change.
Little whirlpools stream by like aimless minnows,
or maybe lemmings on a voyage to nowhere.

The lightness of this lacey band lifts my mood.
The shimmering glints dance along their track
until I notice a vague, but temporary narrowing.
Is my early morning lightshow about to close?

My curiosity sends me to the window for a clue.
I see that the source is the meandering Aberjona.
How could this reclusive river produce such a show,
and how did it arrive at my ceiling arena?

There must be an explanation for this.
Maybe the juxtaposition of the refractions just clicked...
Or maybe the sun conspired with the river
and the early spring shrubs, their leaves still hidden,
to allow each ray to find its way to my waiting stage.

~ Persona ~

Conversations

Mom? We had the baby – a boy.
A boy! How wonderful! Is everybody doing well?
Yes, we are both fine. Can you hear him?
I can. He sounds great! Have you named him?
Yes, his name is Bavo.
Bavo? Can you spell that?
Sure, B-A-V-O.
Okay. Are you good with that?
Yes, in Flemish it means beloved.
It is a fine name, and certainly the only one in his grade.

Boston:
Beautiful baby! What is his name?
Bavo.
No, I mean, what's his real name?

Brooklyn:
Beautiful baby! What is his name?
Bavo.
Oh, what a fantastic name!

One year later, no one could imagine Bavo with any other name.

Fashion Kate

Compared with other little girls,
baby dolls for her just did not rate.
Katherine shied away from bows and curls,
until she fell for Fashion Kate.

A cuddly doll, Fashion Kate could not claim.
Wearing smart clothes was clearly her passion.
Her owner liked that and soon she became
Kate's namesake, foregoing the "Fashion."

Time passed and sports were Kate's prime,
mostly basketball and rowing.
In high school and in college time,
it was in crew she made a showing.

Then modeling became her dream.
Fashion Kate still lives, so it would seem.

Teenage Lament

My survival depends on what?
Being cool, keeping cool, staying cool –
Putting up with, keeping up with, staying up with –
Outlasting the nagging, the threats, the warnings.
When will they stop telling me how to live?

I'm sorry my mother is upset.
It's too bad I'm failing a subject.
I'm bored with the silly groundings
and never-ending advice and admonitions.
It's my life – am I the only one who knows that?

Just chill!

"I Own This Town!"

He was just another kid from the Dorchester projects.
What made Whitey Bulger the master among mobsters?
"Irish godfather," "Robin Hood," the Winter Hill Gang –
"The Most Wanted," second to Osama bin Laden.

His career in crime began at fourteen – armed robbery.
By twenty-six he was doing time in Alcatraz.
Then back to Boston, to round out his resume –
Racketeering, extortion, conspiracy and murder.

Whitey was hand picked by the FBI – Agent John Connolly.
Hoover wanted information to wipe out La Cosa Nostra,
Whitey "talked," while working his own beat – drugs and murder.
Then Connolly became Whitey's informant – protecting and enabling.

Whitey's time ran out in 2011 when he was brought to trial.
Convicted but calm, he flinched when a voice yelled, "Rat!"

Eleanor Reflects

They called me "First Lady of the World" –
a bit flashy, and almost arrogant, I thought,
but frankly, that *is* what I was.
Causes were my cause for existence –
no group escaped my curious and caring nature.
Injustice was my magnet –
no corner of the world eluded me.

At home, I visited the coal mines of West Virginia,
the poverty of Appalachia, the breadlines of New York.
My press corps longed for a day when I was tired.
I reported the terrible conditions of the prisons,
the old-age homes, the tenements.
During the war I went to the battlefields.
Always, – I walked among the people.

Oh, I had my favorites – did you see my picture
when I emerged from the voting booth in 1920?
Yes, I was one of the first women to cast a vote
and a member of the first League of Women Voters.
Teach by example, they said, and so I did.

When the Daughters of the American Revolution
refused Marion Anderson a chance
to sing in Constitution Hall, I resigned from the DAR.
Marion sang at Lincoln Memorial.
Teach by example and walk among the people.

My causes continued: the closing of the Japanese
internment camps, the formation of Israel,
the start of the United Nations. I served there
as a delegate for six years. The Human Rights Commission...
Walk among the people and learn.

But still my approval rating in 1944 was only thirty-six percent!
(Yes, even then the pollsters were busy!)
Some called me traitor, meddler, rattlebrained, and busybody
for my stands on human rights, anti-Semitism, and racism.

Someone once said that I comforted the distressed
and distressed the comfortable ...
to which I replied, "Life has to be lived.
Listen and learn."

On Primrose Hill with Sylvia Plath

I am looking through the window,
Vaguely viewing the damp, dark London street,
While the comforting confines of this room
Surround me like a warm woolen wrap.

These walls once sheltered William Butler Yeats,
who, no doubt, stared through this very window,
perhaps without even seeing the gray dripping streetlights,
or the dull water-color cars slogging through the mist.

So I wait for inspiration on Primrose Hill,
for a rush of insight, a vintage image, a mystical metaphor –
on London streets or maybe the moors of Yorkshire,
far from the fallow fields of Wellesley.

Writing has been the unwavering partnership of my life.
In the beginning it was an eager listener,
one who always cared how I felt.
Then my partner brought me an audience – recognition!

So we are together again, my muse and I –
trudging up Primrose Hill,
not just for the thrill of a perfect phrase.
We seek success and independence!

Come along, my steadfast friend,
Yesterday's sorrow will grow tomorrow's poem,
Or maybe another novel ...
Then we can summer in Devon.

~ Wordplay ~

Where Have All My Metaphors Gone?

Right now my metaphors are looking elsewhere
for a big concept in search of an analogy.
The similes no longer care about comparing,
nor do they *like* each other *as* they should.
Meanwhile my alliterations are all meeting
in that magnificent mall in Minneapolis, Minnesota.
The repetitions are being bored on the shores of Bora Bora,
while my rhymes are wining and dining in Hong Kong.
The couplets are skipping away, hand in hand,
to put the proper ending on someone else's sonnet.
Even my themes with their life-changing experiences
are experiencing the dreaded change-of-life!
Which leaves me alone with a blank sheet of paper ...
My muse is not amused.

Triolets

Ballerina

Poised to perform, she will pose,
Pink leotard, tutu, and tights.
Too young to be on her toes,
Poised to perform, she will pose,
Waiting for the moment she goes
On stage, on this night of nights.
Poised to perform, she will pose
Pink leotard, tutu, and tights.

Moviescape

Woody Allen will always be the same
He's still reinventing Annie Hall
The Coen brothers will play a quirky game
Woody Allen is always the same.
Robert deNiro remains a great name
And Meryl Streep will always stand tall
Woody Allen will always be the same
He's still reinventing Annie Hall.

Outing Emily

Emily Dickinson wanted to be alone
Just to be alone and dress in white
So why for gossip does the public moan?
Emily Dickinson wanted to be alone.
Romance with Higgenbottom is the latest tome
Though evidence has proven quite slight
Emily Dickinson wanted to be alone
Just to be alone and dress in white.

Continued on next page

Watching the Puppet

We watch the puppet show to spot the strings,
Hoping for a new Pinocchio,
Wishing this time he's sprout some wings-
We watch the puppet show to spot the strings.
Knowing that life seldom brings such things,
And would cause immense imbroglio.
We watch the puppet show to spot the strings,
Still hoping for a new Pinocchio.

The Favored Sight

The favored sight is that which disappears
My mother standing at the oval door-
We drive away, the family hiding tears
The favored sight is that which disappears
Our visits and vacations through the years,
Though they were many, always cried for more.
The favored sight is that which disappears –
My mother standing at the oval door.

The Key to Tai Chi

Where can I find the key to Tai Chi?
When will it all make sense?
Each graceful movement, so lovely to see
Where can I find the key to Tai Chi?
I am looking for some continuity
The lack of which makes me quite tense
Where can I find the key to Tai Chi?
When will it all make sense?

Stopped by Words
Apologies to Robert Frost

Whose words these are I think I know –
whose poems delude his readers so.
His images run through his head,
sometimes not knowing where to go.

His readers all must carefully tread
to eke out each affected thread,
between his musings, much expressed,
where thought and pen are hardly wed.

If whimsy is the reader's quest,
or just a little bit of jest,
cliches from all the lines endure,
worn out drollery at its best.

Deliver me from odes obscure;
bring me the message, clear and pure.

Almost Anyone
Acclaiming the "A"

Almost anyone is accepted.
All boast an admiration for art.
Art appreciators plod purposefully, or
Amble aimlessly.
Actual artists hover hopefully, trying to be nonchalant.
Anxious amateurs cluster with capable contenders.
Apparent authorities mingle with pretentious poseurs.

Anticipate! Demonstrate! Celebrate!
Advertise your skill! Merchandise at will!
Applause arrives in many modes, but –
Always be steeled for silence.

Retrograde Reincarnation
A Rhyme Resplendent with R's

Remembering, recalling moments past,
enriching remnants of a time gone by,
roaming through the rights and wrongs received,
rifling through reveling and regret –
reasons these to write and reminisce.

Roses reap reminders of romance.
Rhetoric derails or rhapsodizes.
Aromas render a range of recollections,
arising from repeated recipes.
(Ribs and roasts receive resounding raves.)

So, raid your inner retrospective self.
Revisit, relish, relate, and resurrect!
Reclaim your past, be ready to restore.
Wrap yourself in regal robes of yore.
Reincarnate the 'you' that went before.

The Duplicity of Monotony

The importance of monotony is questionable.
Who would pursue it with purposeful tenacity?
No one seeking variety or frivolity –
No one studying psychology or biology –
No one attuned to polygamy or diversity.
Indeed, its fidelity seems to be with boredom.

For total veracity, let me change my mind.
Consistency and conformity are admirable,
but may be deemed monotonous by some.
Insomniacs crave the redundancy of silence.
Stability and civility calmly co-exist.
Equality revels in its constancy.
Can the importance of monotony lie in its dichotomy?

Triskaidekaphobia

Fear of the number 13

Thirteen – it only expresses an amount –
one more than twelve – a baker's dozen.
What has made it so much maligned?
Some say it's the Last Supper – the fateful thirteen
around the table – then one left, and there were twelve.
Thirteen full moons in one year – review your calendar
and it will show twelve months of bad luck – always.
Beware of Friday the 13th – a doctor's appointment
on that day assures an unfortunate diagnosis.
A gathering of thirteen means one less next year.

But remember – thirteen stripes in the flag stand for
our thirteen colonies – Apollo 13 failed, but –
the crew returned safely. Thirteen is a prime number
and the smallest number with eight letters.
So what's in a number?

Fading Light

From mind's murky mist there bounds a thought
so bright, an idea all aglow with inner light,
a concept so unique, so promising,
conceived today to be my prodigy.
From this idea, actions will make way,
I muse – at mindplay, letting thoughts stray,
eagerly hoping for some recognition
afforded to my promising creation.

But wait! I think I've walked this way before.
My prodigy may prove just wan and weak.
A thought that often leads to nothing more –
and thus the celebration that I seek
will fade away – no bright light to restore.
And I'll extol the merits of the meek.

Seeking the Light

Many light years ago,
I dreamed of writing light comedy.
I wanted to be a highlight in the world of humor.

I labored in my lonely, lackluster room,
hunkering beneath a solitary light bulb
from dawn till twilight.

It was difficult to be lighthearted.
The very effort almost made me lightheaded.
Inspiration was elusive, or worse – absent.

Then I heard a voice saying, "You must lighten up!"
It hit me like a bolt of lightning.
And suddenly I was enlightened!

Ideas tripped lightly into my mind.
Humor, drollery, wit descended on me.
I was truly beginning to see the light!

Now I delight in bringing mirth to the earth ...
I feel a lightness of being, lifted by laughter.
Perhaps my levity has lightened a corner of your life.

Waves

Merciless waves pound the wharf,
angry arcs whipping, ripping, mocking,
each repetition unstoppable, unrelenting, unraveling.

Against this intensity, a large boat pushes out to sea –
two adverse forces, each resolute, unwavering,
two diverse courses, preordained and unalterable.

The large boat invades the breaking waves – ravaging, savaging,
destroying what had been, transforming the seascape,
changing forever what had only yesterday been real.

While on the wharf, a lone soul watches the large boat,
waves to one who is farther away with each hateful wave
and knows the waves of sadness drowning her
will persist, like the grave waves that pound the waiting shore.

Thanks for the Memories

A large sun-filled room,
a parade of people entering –
wheelchairs, walkers, and some canes,
easing into easy chairs
watching, waiting, anticipating.
When the pianist finally arrives – rumpled, yet resolute,
the silent keyboard comes alive.
The man is good!
Old standards fill the room.
Solemn faces yield to slow smiles.
Melodies beget memories, and
is that humming in the background?

You're remembering Those Foolish Things,
basking under Blue Skies
and smarting when Smoke Gets in Your Eyes.
Someone said It Had to be You and
there you were, Over the Rainbow.
A smattering of Stardust,
then suddenly it was The Last Dance.
I'll See You in My Dreams.